Bible sleuth

Old Testament

ILLUSTRATED BY
JOSÉ PÉREZ MONTERO

TYNDALE
KIDS

Tyndale House Publishers, Inc.
Carol Stream, IL

Hi there! I'm Mike. I love adventures and going back in time. I'm especially fond of going back in biblical times and witnessing some of the most exciting events in history. Are you good at finding things? If you are, I'd love to bring you along on another adventure. We'll do some investigating, and you'll be an expert Bible Sleuth by the end of our journey.

Here are a few things you should know before we go: as you read the stories, try to find the pictures in the sidebar in each scene. When you find each clue, you'll learn a little more about the colorful, dramatic, and sometimes chaotic biblical world. You'll see funny or surprising things along the way—some will make you laugh; others might make your jaw drop. It's all part of the fun as we go through the Old Testament together.

God Creates the Animals

After God had created the earth, He said, "Let the earth be filled with animals." So God made tame animals, small crawling animals, and wild animals of all shapes and sizes. When God saw all the animals He created, He said, "It is good." *See Genesis 1:24-25.*

Noah Builds the Ark

God told Noah, "All the people on earth have become evil. Build a boat for your family because I am going to flood the earth and destroy all living things. But you will be safe in the boat. Also bring two of every animal on the boat to keep them alive." Noah did everything God commanded. *See Genesis 6:13-22.*

Look for:

5

Arguing at the Tower of Babel

There was a time when everyone spoke the same language, and they decided to make a tower that reached the sky so they would become famous. God said, "They are united because they speak the same language. They could accomplish anything they want." So God mixed up their language and scattered them over the world.   *See Genesis 11:1-9.*

The Israelites Cry in Egypt

The people of Israel lived in Egypt. There were so many Israelites that the king of Egypt was afraid they might fight against the Egyptians. So the Egyptians made slaves out of the Israelites, forcing them to work hard in the Egyptians' fields and build their cities. *See Exodus 1:7-14.*

Look for:

Crossing the Red Sea

Moses led the Israelites out of Egypt, but the Egyptians chased after them, trying to bring them back to Egypt. When the people came to the Red Sea, Moses held up his hand and God parted the waters. The Egyptians followed them into the sea, but after the Israelites crossed to the other side, God let the waters crash over the Egyptians. *See Exodus 14:21-30.*

Eating Manna in the Desert

While the Israelites were traveling, God heard them grumble about their hunger. So He sent birds each evening so they would have meat, and He sent manna each morning, which was like bread. Moses told them God had provided this food, and they should each gather enough for their families.

See Exodus 16:12-16.

13

War against the Amalekites

The Amalekites came and attacked the Israelites. During the battle, Moses, Aaron, and Hur went to a hill nearby, and Moses held up his hands and prayed to God. If he let his hands down, the Amalekites would win, but if he held them up, the Israelites would win. Aaron and Hur helped Moses hold up his hands, and the Israelites won the war!

See Exodus 17:8-13.

Look for:

15

The Fall of Jericho

God had given the Israelites the city of Jericho, but it was surrounded by walls. God said to Joshua, "March around the city with your army once each day for six days. On the seventh day, march around it seven times. Have the priests blow their trumpets and the people shout, and the walls will fall down." Joshua did everything God asked, and the walls fell! The Israelites ran into the city and defeated Jericho's army. *See Joshua 6:1-20.*

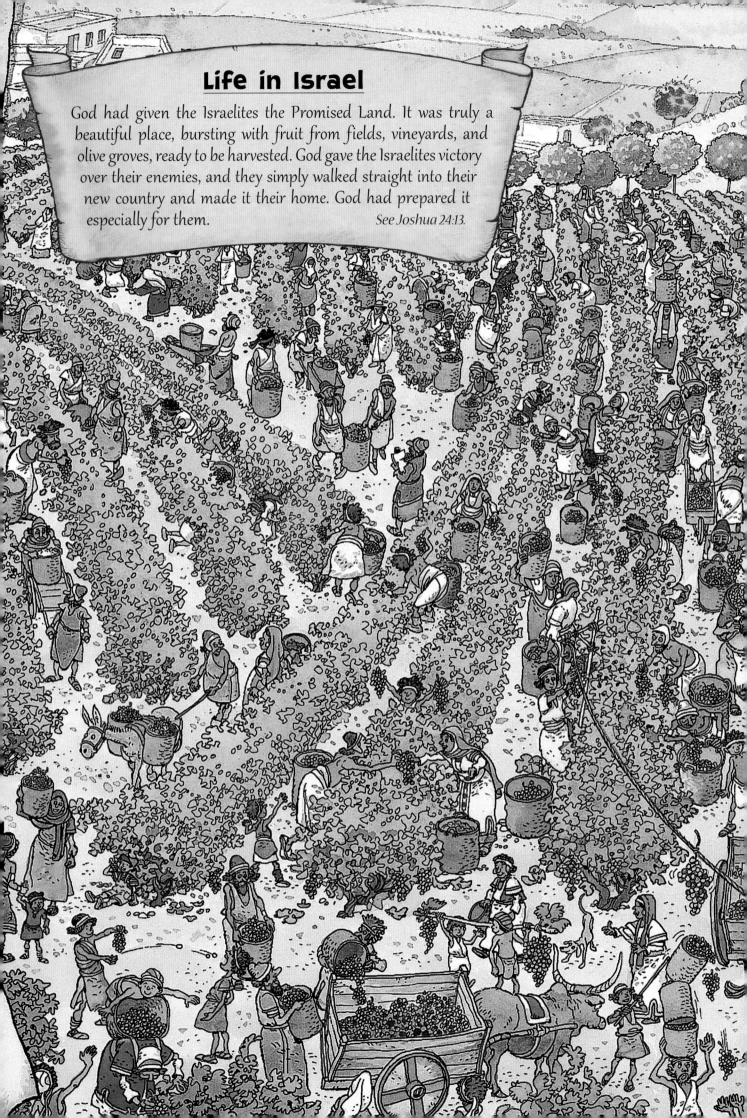

Life in Israel

God had given the Israelites the Promised Land. It was truly a beautiful place, bursting with fruit from fields, vineyards, and olive groves, ready to be harvested. God gave the Israelites victory over their enemies, and they simply walked straight into their new country and made it their home. God had prepared it especially for them.

See Joshua 24:13.

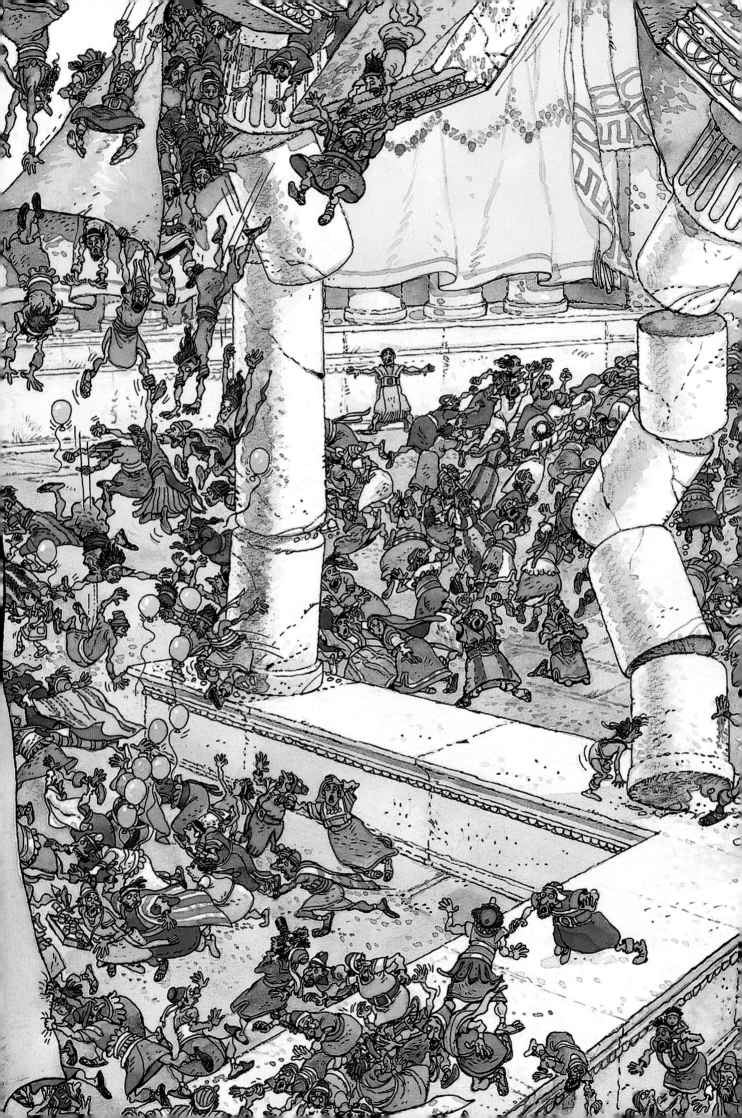

Samson's Story

The Philistine kings gathered to thank their god, Dagon, for helping them capture Samson, the Israelites' hero and protector. One day, they brought Samson out to make fun of him; then they stood him between two pillars that held up Dagon's temple. Samson prayed, "God, please give me strength just one more time." He pushed the pillars as hard as he could. They broke and the temple crashed to the ground. For the last time in his life, Samson defeated his enemies with the help of God.

See Judges 16:23-30.

Look for:

David Fights Goliath

Goliath challenged the Israelites: "Send one man to fight me. If I win, you will become our slaves. If you win, we will become your slaves." The Israelites were terrified of Goliath, but David said, "I'll fight him!" Then, facing the giant with only a slingshot, David yelled, "You fight me with sword and spear, but I fight you in the name of the Lord!" As Goliath cursed and ridiculed him, David ran at Goliath and slung a stone from his slingshot. It hit Goliath hard, and he fell to the ground. God gave David and the Israelite army the victory!   *See 1 Samuel 17:8-54.*

Look for:

23

David Brings the Ark of the Covenant

The Ark of the Covenant, which held the Ten Commandments, had been stolen by the Philistines and had been missing from Jerusalem for several years. Now King David was determined to bring the Ark back. After one failed attempt, he was finally able to bring it back where it belonged. As the priests carried it into Jerusalem, many Israelites played instruments, and David danced with all his might before God. David was so happy to finally have the Ark of the Covenant back.

See 2 Samuel 6:1-19.

Look for:

Building God's Temple

Four hundred eighty years after the Israelites had left their lives of slavery in Egypt, Solomon, the son of David, started to build the house of the Lord—the beautiful Temple in Jerusalem. He made sure the workers built it exactly right. God promised His people, "Obey My laws and commands, and I will live in this Temple and bless you and the land in which you live." Solomon used the finest materials, and after seven years, it was finally finished. They had built a house for God.   *See 1 Kings 6.*

Look for:

Jerusalem's Walls

The Israelites were captured by their enemies, and God finally led them home. After many years and wars, the walls surrounding Jerusalem had crumbled. God put Nehemiah in charge of rebuilding them. God gave Nehemiah a great plan. Each person in Jerusalem would work on the section of the wall that was closest to where they lived. With this plan, the Israelites rebuilt the mighty walls of Jerusalem in only fifty-two days.   *See Nehemiah 2–3; 6:15-16.*

Visit Tyndale's website for kids at www.tyndale.com/kids.

TYNDALE is a registered trademark of Tyndale House Publishers, Inc. The Tyndale Kids logo is a trademark of Tyndale House Publishers, Inc.

Bible Sleuth: Old Testament

Original edition published in Denmark under the title *Bible Detective* by Scandinavia Publishing House, Copenhagen, Denmark.

Previously published as *Bible Detective: Looking for God's People* (ISBN 9788771328332) and *Bible Detective: Looking for the Promised Land* (ISBN 9788771328349) by Scandinavia Publishing House. First printing by Tyndale House Publishers, Inc., in 2017.

Text by Vanessa Carroll

Designed by Gao Hanyu, Li Dan

Illustrated by José Pérez Montero.

Edited by Cecilie Fodor

For manufacturing information regarding this product, please call 1-800-323-9400.

ISBN 978-1-4964-2244-6
Printed in China
23   22   21   20   19   18   17
7   6   5   4   3   2   1